T0345678

3

2ND EDITION
BIG TV WORKBOOK

Pearson Education Limited
KAO Two
KAO Park
Harlow
Essex CM17 9NA
England
and Associated Companies throughout the world.

www.English.com/BigEnglish2

© Pearson Education Limited 2017

First published 2017
ISBN: 978-1-292-20360-7
Set in Heinemann Roman
Printed in Italy by L.E.G.O. S.p.A.

Acknowledgements
The publisher would like to thank the following for their kind permission to reproduce their photographs:

(Key: b-bottom; c-centre; l-left; r-right; t-top)

123RF.com: 11 (station), 15cl, Andegro4ka 19t (snow leopard), Aquafun 16 (frogfish), 18t (frogfish), 18b, Avelkrieg 27t (smell), Bachol2345 28b (bake), Steve Ball 17 (paw prints), 18t (paw prints), Boule13 28t (crack), Brgfx 7c (Ben), 7c (Jerry), 7c (Luis), 7c (Sandy), 7c (Yanny), Chamillewhite 32 (exercise), Weerachat Chatroopamai 15tl, Courtyardpix 35br, Daviden 12/2, 14br, Dazdraperma 27t (dog), Dolgachov 7bl, 11br, Gekaskr 5br, 9br, Gelpi 19bl, 39br, Graphicbee 35t (Julia), Herjua 5 (dirt), Iimages 31t (Donna), 31t (Jan), 31t (Johnny), 31t (Scott), Images 25br (Illustration), Jehsomwang 37br (illustration), Joruba 4/6, K. Thalhofer 12/3, Kittasgraphics 19t (octopus), Evgenii Komissarov 23t, Andrei Krauchuk 11 (Amanda), 11 (Stephen), Kurhan 9 (c), Oksana Kuzmina 32 (diet), Lammeyer 17br, Lightwise 5 (bacteria), Pavel Losevsky 11 (monorail), 24 (hear), 26t (listen), Anton Lunkov 19t (fish), Macrovector 39cl (gallery), Makasanaphoto 22, Anastasiia Malysheva 35t (played tennis), Margouillat 31c (Easter Eggs), Trevor William Mayes 14b, Michaeljung 39bl, Teguh Mujiono 7 (Ben), 7 (Jerry), 7 (Luis), 7 (Sandy), 7 (Yanny), 17br (illustration), 33bc (illustration), 35t (Marco), Duncan Noakes 12/6, 14tc, Nobilior 20 (icy), David Novi 10b, Iryna Novytsky 13 (camel), 13 (dog), 13 (dolphin), 13 (elephant), 13 (horse), 13 (sheep), Nyul 24 (touch), Yana Ogonkova 8/5, Mikhaylov Oleg 4/5, Patl38241 33bc, Andrey Pavlov 5br (Illustration), Felix Pergande 27t (radar), Anastasija Popova 15b, Aleksandr Popovskiy 11 (underground train), Nataliia Prokofyeva 4/1, Prometeus 35bl, Rabbit75123 36 (cathedral), Bernard Rabone 11 (elevated train), Rilueda 32 (bunk beds), 34t (bunk beds), Rndms 5 (hot springs), Sam74100 7br, 11bl, Ksenya Savva 35c, Sborisov 20 (sunny), Dmitriy Shironosov 4/7, Sutiporn Somnam 13tl, 14bl, Stnazkul 21bl, Stocksolutions 29b, Nadzeya Varovich 27t (bat), Paul Vinten 24 (sonar), Wavebreak Media Ltd 4/4, Hongqi Zhang 15tr, Zsooofija 9br (illustration); **Pearson Education Ltd:** Jon Barlow 27br, Trevor Clifford 23bl, Amit John 35t (went to bed), Coleman Yuen. Pearson Education Asia Ltd 17 (pebble), 28b (fry), Pearson Education Ltd 27t (sonar), Pradip Kumar Bhowal. Pearson India Education Services Pvt. Ltd 27 (dolphin), 35t (healthy food), Ratan Mani Banerjee. Pearson India Education Services Pvt. Ltd 35t (Juan), 39cl (park), Tudor Photography 9 (a), 32 (plants), 34t (plants), Debbie Rowe 8/3, 9 (b), 10t (tube train), 36 (church), 36 (park), Ruth Thomlevold 39t (Cleo), 39t (Kevin), 39t (Marta), 39t (Mickey), Utsav Academy and Art Studio. Pearson India Education Services Pvt. Ltd 19t (cuttlefish); **Shutterstock.com:** 2238920 34b, Aletia 15cr, Amble Design 20 (stormy), Auremar 8/8, Alexandru Axon 16 (cuttlefish), 18t (cuttlefish), Balounm 38, Lara Barrett 37 (b), Bennyartist 16 (shrimp), Mikkel Bigandt 14tr, Bikeriderlondon 36 (exhibition), Olesia Bilkei 20 (warm), Bitt24 31c (eggs), Blacqbook 24 (see), 26t (see), Bochkarev Photography 29tc, 31c (popcorn), BORTEL Pavel - Pavelmidi 16 (goat), Victor Brave 35t (Sarah), Brocreative 13tr, Sergiy Bykhunenko 37br, D. Kucharski K. Kucharska 5 (insects), Comaniciu Dan 36 (gallery), Danaij 28b (make), Yulia Davidovich 33t (healthy), Andy Dean Photography 27bl, Songquan Deng 20 (freezing), Dennis W Donohue 16 (snow leopard), Thierry Duran 16 (octopus), 18t (octopus), ElenaShow 39cr (theatre), Anna Elizabeth photography 13tc, 14tl, Elnur 37 (a), Ew Chee Guan 25br, G. K. 20 (rainy), Gelpi JM 24 (taste), Mandy Godbehear 32 (fresh air), 34t (fresh air), Goodluz 12/1, Joe Gough 33t (ready-made), 34t (ready-made), Guas 21tr, HABRDA 20 (snowy), Jorg Hackemann 8/7, Rob Hainer 16 (gorilla), Alison Hancock 32 (garden), Haraldmuc 17 (shells), 18t (shells), Robert Hoetink 20 (windy), Fat Jackey 8/4, Natalie Jean 17 (seaweed), Jirsak 24 (radar), Cathy Keifer 16 (chameleon), 18t (chameleon), Robert Kneschke 28t (cook), l i g h t p o e t 8/6, 10t (passenger), Andrew Lever 12/5, LooksLikeLisa 4/2, LoopAll 35t (fresh air), Mamahoohooba 8/2, 10t (elevated train), Maridav 33t (fit), Matt9122 26b, V. J. Matthew 21tl, Olga Miltsova 5 (minerals), Monkey Business Images 36 (museum), Juriah Mosin 24 (smell), 26t (smelll), Sergey Novikov 31br, Four Oaks 6, Olena I 33t (unhealthy), Oliveromg 37 (c), Tyler Olson 30, Anna Om 19br, phoelixDE 21b, Pixelman 29tr, David Pruter 12/4, Francesco Scatena 21br, Ian Scott 25 (c), 26t (hammerhead shark), Mihai Simonia 36 (theatre), Orlando_Stocker 32 (exhaust fumes), 34t (exhaust fumes), Tomacco 39cr (church), Rudy Umans 8/1, 10t (monorail), Vasyliuk 10t (model train), Roman Vintonyak 25 (a), Vkilikov 25 (b), 26t (dolphins), Kirsanov Valeriy Vladimirovich 25 (d), 26t (bat), Valentyn Volkov 32 (vegetables), Tatyana Vyc 23br, Tom Wang 31bl, Wavebreakmedia 4/3, 28t (eat), 32 (race), 34t (race), Wiktory 29tl, 31c (porridge)

All other images © Pearson Education

Contents

Staying Clean

Before You Watch

I will learn about keeping clean and healthy.

1 **Listen, look, and say.**

1 take a shower

2 wash your hands

3 brush your teeth

4 keep clean

5 have a bath

6 sneeze into your hands

7 don't pass on germs

2 **Read and complete.**

pass	wash	keep	take	brush	sneeze

a Please _____ your hands before dinner.

b Don't forget to _____ your teeth before bed.

c Try not to _____ on your germs if you are sick.

d _____ a shower every morning.

e _____ into your hands or into a tissue.

f There are lots of ways to _____ clean every day.

3 Listen, look, and say.

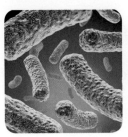    

bacteria   dirt   hot spring   insects   minerals

4 What do you do to keep clean? Ask and answer with a partner. Draw.

5 ▶(v1) **Watch. Check (✓) what you hear or see.**

- ☐ keep clean
- ☐ have a bath
- ☐ take a shower
- ☐ brush teeth
- ☐ pass on germs
- ☐ wash our hands
- ☐ bacteria
- ☐ dirt

6 ▶(v1) **Watch again. Write True or False.**

a Children use a dance to remember how to wash their hands. _____

b Crocodiles have to keep their teeth clean. _____

c Elephants love to brush their teeth. _____

d Ancient Romans used hot springs to have a bath. _____

e Water with minerals isn't healthy. _____

f People don't use Roman baths today. _____

7 **Read and circle. Then listen and check.**

Crocodiles and sea lions have their teeth cleaned to remove **bacteria / minerals**. This is just like humans. Elephants love to have **baths / showers**. Elephants often climb into water to wash away dirt and remove **bacteria / insects** from their skin. The elephants also enjoy **fighting / cleaning** each other, relaxing, and playing in the bath. It's a **big / social** event!

8 **Follow the lines. Ask and answer with a partner.**

9 **Write the words in order and match.**
Then listen and check.

a [every - What - she - morning - does - do?]   [I have a bath.]

What does she do every morning?

b [he - do - breakfast - does - What - after?]   [She has a shower.]

c [every - What - do - evening - you - do?]   [He brushes his teeth.]

THINK BIG

Why is it good to wash our hands before we eat?
What other times do we need to wash our hands?

2 Trains

I will learn about different trains.

1 Listen, look, and say.

| 1 | monorail

| 2 | elevated train

| 3 | underground train

| 4 | railway

| 5 | ticket

| 6 | passenger

| 7 | station

| 8 | ticket inspector

2 Read and complete.

passengers   station   elevated   underground   inspector   ticket

a For trains to Cityville, please buy a _____ on Platform 5.

b There is a ticket _____ on all trains.

c _____ trains run above ground level. You can often see them in cities.

d Traveling by bus is fun, but the _____ train is faster.

e All _____ should look after their own bags.

f This _____ closes at midnight.

3 **Match. Then listen and check.**

a

b

c

(the Tube)   (tourists)   (model train)

4 **What transportation do you have in your city? Draw. Then ask and answer with a partner.**

5 **Watch. What do you hear or see? Number the pictures in order, 1 to 5.**

6 ▶ⱽ² **Watch again. Then read and write.**

a Is there a monorail in Chicago?

_____

b What unusual type of transportation is there in Seattle?

_____

c Where can you travel on the Tube?

_____

d Where can you see a chocolate train?

_____

7 **Read and complete. Then listen and check.**

tickets	chocolate	underground	railway	model

In Budapest, there's a special children's _____. The full-size trains run through the forest in Buda and are staffed almost entirely by children. They inspect _____, make the announcements, and handle sales.

John Poley drove the London _____, usually known as the Tube, for many years. Now, John has his own _____ version at home. In Belgium, there's the longest _____ train ever built. It may be slow, but it's a sweet ride!

8 **Follow the map. Ask and answer with a partner.**

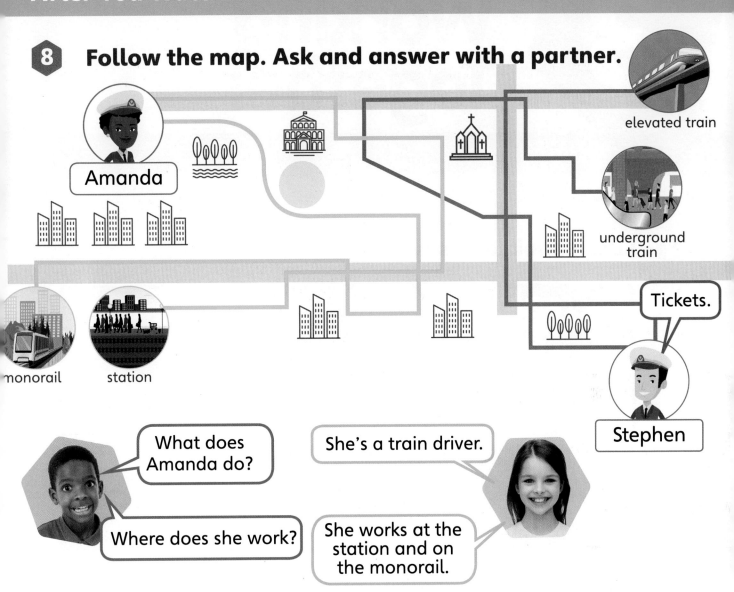

Amanda

elevated train

underground train

Tickets.

monorail   station

Stephen

What does Amanda do?

She's a train driver.

Where does she work?

She works at the station and on the monorail.

9 **Write questions. Then listen and check.**

a <u>What does Rosy do?</u>   Rosy is a ticket inspector.

b _____? Jack works at the station.

c _____? Heather and Alfie are train drivers.

d _____? Mae works on the monorail.

THINK BIG **Why is it good to travel by train?**

Working Together

I will learn about working with animals.

1 🎧 **Listen, look, and say.**

1 work with

2 trust

3 jump out of

4 feed

5 communicate with

6 develop a bond with

2 **Choose words from 1. Write.**

a I love to _____ my classmates. We make a good team.

b I need to _____ my dog three times a day. He is always hungry.

c I am afraid to _____ an airplane!

d We _____ other people by talking.

e I _____ my teacher. She always helps me.

🎧 3 Listen, look, and say.

mahout

horse whisperer

farmer

4 Read. Ask and answer with a partner.

How do people work with these animals?

What jobs do they do?

Which animals would you like to work with? Why?

elephant

dog

dolphin

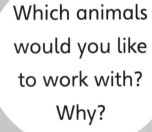
horse

sheep

camel

5 ▶ v3 **Watch. What do you hear or see?**
Number the pictures in order, 1 to 5.

6 ▶ v3 **Watch again. Write True or False.**

a The mahouts work closely with their dogs. _____

b The farmer from England works with a dog. _____

c In New York, the miniature horse visits hospitals. _____

d The horse whisperer is from Thailand. _____

e The horses don't trust the horse whisperer. _____

7 🎧 **Read and circle. Then listen and check.**

In Thailand, people are celebrating the birth of two baby **elephants / horses**. The baby elephants can meet the people who live with them. They are called **mahouts / farmers**. Each mahout develops a close **job / bond** with one elephant.

In England, the **farmer / whisperer** works with his dog to herd **dogs / sheep**. And his dog loves riding in the farmer's aircraft.

8 **Look and choose. Then ask and answer with a partner.**

mahout

communicate with

develop a bond with

feed

work with

farmer

What does the mahout have to do?

He has to feed the elephants.

9 13 **Read, circle, and write. Then listen and check.**

Job file: Working as a horse whisperer

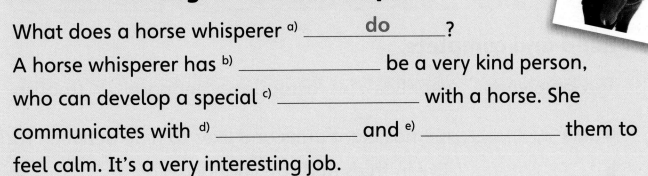

What does a horse whisperer a) _____do_____?
A horse whisperer has b) _____ be a very kind person,
who can develop a special c) _____ with a horse. She
communicates with d) _____ and e) _____ them to
feel calm. It's a very interesting job.

a (do)/ does / make	**c** jump / bond / work	**e** helps / helped / helping
b with / to / not	**d** dolphins / dogs / horses	

THINK BIG

How can we look after animals?

Hidden Animals

I will learn about how animals hide.

14

1 **Listen, number, and say.**

| | goat | | gorilla | | frogfish | | cuttlefish |

| | octopus | | shrimp | | snow leopard | | chameleon |

2 **Read and complete.**

| chameleons | gorillas | octopus | leopard | frogfish |

a An _____ has eight arms and likes to hide between rocks.

b _____ live in trees and can change color.

c A snow _____ looks the same as the rocks and snow around it.

d _____ live at the bottom of the sea and hide in seaweed.

e _____ live in big family groups.

3 **Listen, look, and say.**

seaweed

pebble

shells

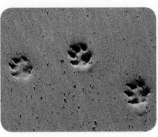
paw prints

4 **What animals are hiding in your neighborhood? Ask and answer with a partner. Draw.**

5 **Watch. What do you hear or see? Number the pictures in order, 1 to 6.**

6 **Watch again. Answer the questions.**

a What do the cuttlefish look like?

_____

b Is the octopus good at hiding inside its environment?

_____

c How do the men find the snow leopard?

_____

d Which animal can change the color of its skin?

_____

7 **Read and complete. Then listen and check.**

| fish | seaweed | frogfish | swim | quickly |

The _____ is a master of camouflage.

It doesn't _____ often. It hides inside

_____ and uses its fins to hold on. It's

really well disguised. When a shrimp or

small _____ comes along, the frogfish

moves _____ and eats it.

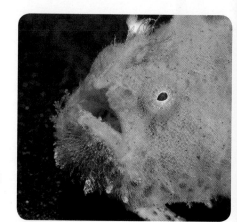

8 **Match. Ask and answer with a partner.**

| looks like snow | hides among the seaweed | hides inside places | changes color |

How does the octopus hide?

It hides inside places.

17

9 **Write the words in order and match. Then listen and check.**

a does - frogfish - the - Where - hide?

Where does the frogfish hide?
_____

It looks like the rocks where it lives.

b leopard - hide - the - How - does - snow?

_____

They blend in with their environment.

c octopus - How - the - hide - does?

_____

It hides among seaweed.

d do - chameleons - How - hide?

_____

It hides under things.

THINK BIG

Which animals hide best? Ask your classmates.

5 Extreme Weather

Before You Watch

I will learn about different kinds of weather.

18
1 Listen, number, and say.

☐ snowy

☐ rainy

☐ stormy

☐ sunny

☐ icy

☐ windy

☐ freezing

☐ warm

2 Read and complete.

| icy | windy | rainy | snowy | warm |

a When the weather is _____, our teacher takes us outside.

b I like playing with my kite on a _____ day.

c I love _____ weather because I can go sledding with my friends.

d Break time will be inside if it is _____ and wet outside.

e If average temperatures are very low, the streets may be _____.

3 Look, read, and complete the weather expressions. Then listen and check.

sunny	deep	extreme	warm

a _____ snow

b _____ hat

c _____ storm

d _____ day

4 What's your favorite type of weather? Ask your classmates. Make a chart.

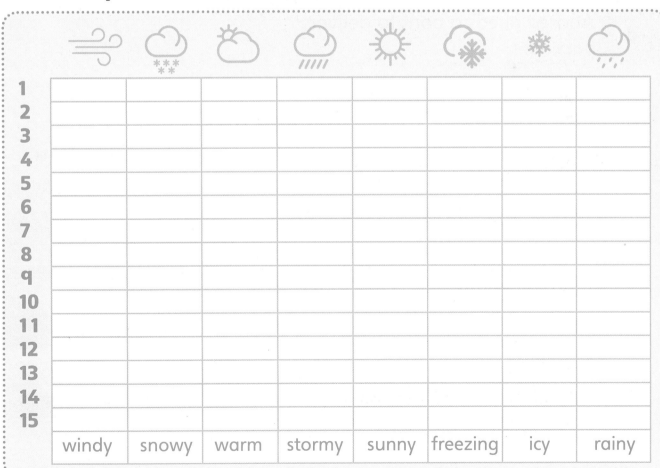

	windy	snowy	warm	stormy	sunny	freezing	icy	rainy
1								
2								
3								
4								
5								
6								
7								
8								
9								
10								
11								
12								
13								
14								
15								

BIG tv

5 ▶ⓥ5 Watch. Check (✓) what you hear or see.

☐ sunny ☐ extreme storm ☐ rainy

☐ stormy ☐ freezing ☐ deep snow

6 ▶ⓥ5 Watch again. Check (✓) the correct places.

		Germany	Russia	Alaska	Croatia
a	Irina has a sled to deliver mail.				
b	Zoltan uses a horse to carry the shopping.				
c	Tod is bringing pizzas on his plane.				
d	Andrea needs a boat to deliver packages.				

🎧20 7 Read and circle. Then listen and check.

If average temperatures are very low, a **sled / storm** may be a good idea. Irina, a **pizza / mail** carrier in Russia, has one ready for her daily delivery of post. However, even a sled would fail in this village in Croatia. The place has been cut off by an **extreme / deep** storm.

To get the shopping, Zoltan needs more than a **warm / hot** hat and gloves. He needs a new way to travel.

8 **Look at the weather on Wednesday in these countries. Ask and answer with a partner.**

China	India	the UK	Denmark	the USA	Siberia	Germany

What was the weather like in China on Wednesday?

It was snowy.

9 **Read and complete. Write a, b, c, or d. Then listen and check.**

Jackie: I'm so happy that it's sunny today!

Fred: ___c___

Jackie: What a difference! Yesterday it was so cold!

Fred: _____

Jackie: I know! And in the afternoon it was very snowy.

Fred: _____

Jackie: That's true, but it's warm and windy today instead.

Fred: _____

Jackie: Great idea, Fred. Let's go!

a	It wasn't cold, it was freezing!	**c**	Me too! It's such a nice day, not like yesterday.
b	It was good weather for sledding.	**d**	It's a great day for flying kites.

What kind of weather do you have in your area?

6 The Senses

1 **Listen, number, and say.**

see

hear

taste

smell

touch

radar

sonar

2 **Choose words from 1. Write.**

a When you _____ something, you are using your sight.

b Those cookies _____ really good when you bite them.

c Some animals, like dolphins, use _____ in the sea to find food.

d You use your ears to _____.

e These flowers _____ very nice.

3 **Match. Then listen and check.**

a   b   c   d

(hammerhead shark)   (stingray)   (bat)   (bottlenose dolphin)

4 **What special sense would you like to have? Why?**
Ask and answer with a partner.

super
sense of smell

sonar

radar

can see
in the dark

5 ▶ v6 **Watch. What do you hear or see?**
Number the pictures in order, 1 to 6.

6 ▶ v6 **Watch again. Answer the questions.**

a Why are they called hammerhead sharks? _____

b When do hammerhead sharks hunt? _____

c Do bats have sensitive ears? _____

d Why do dolphins use sonar? _____

e How does the dog detect diseases? _____

7 **Read and complete. Then listen and check.**

| see | radar | eyes | hear | ears |

Because of the position of their _____,
hammerhead sharks are able to _____ above
and below themselves at the same time!

Bats use a type of _____ to detect prey. This
is why bats have particularly sensitive _____. Bats are able to
_____ where their prey is. Bats need super ears to find prey in
the dark.

8 **What can they do to find food? Match. Then ask and answer with a partner.**

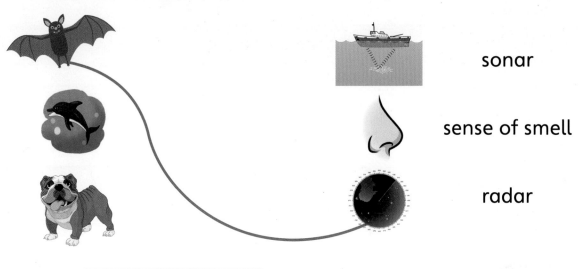

sonar

sense of smell

radar

What can bats do to find food?

They can use their radar.

9 **Read and match.**

a | Bats can hear well, but they can't see very well.

b | Dogs have a good sense of smell.

c | Hammerhead sharks have eyes far apart.

d | Bottlenose dolphins use their special sense to hunt.

They use sonar to find fish!

They use radar to hunt.

They use their noses to find food.

They are able to see above and below themselves at the same time.

THINK BIG

Which sense is the most useful? Have a class vote.

What's Cooking?

I will learn about cooking.

 1 **Listen, number, and say.**

☐ eat

☐ cook

☐ crack

☐ fry

☐ bake

☐ make

2 **Read and complete.**

crack	eat	bake	fry	make

a It's easy to _____ my special omelet.

b First, you need to _____ the eggs.

c You then need to _____ the egg and ingredients in a pan.

d Finally, you _____ this delicious meal!

e My dad loves to _____. His favorite recipe is chocolate cake.

3 Listen, look, and say.

porridge   popcorn   fried egg

4 What can you cook? Write the recipe.

Ingredients

Method

5 ▶(V7) **Watch. Check (✓) what you hear or see.**

- ☐ cook
- ☐ eat
- ☐ apple
- ☐ bread
- ☐ crack
- ☐ broken eggs
- ☐ fried egg
- ☐ make

6 ▶(V7) **Watch again. Write True or False.**

a The hens in the schoolyard eat popcorn. _____

b The schoolyard chickens produce six eggs per day. _____

c You can use a knife or a fork to crack an egg. _____

d You'll need juice to make a fried egg. _____

e The 2000kg egg is made of fruit. _____

7 **Read and circle. Then listen and check.**

If you buy eggs in a shop, don't forget to check for **broken / clean** eggs.

Once you have your eggs, the first step is to **smash / crack** them into a bowl. Some people use a fork or a knife, but in this **baking / science** class, they suggest you use another **person / egg**. Give it a try!

If you choose to make a **chocolate / fried** egg, you'll need some oil in a frying pan and a spatula.

8 Follow the lines. Ask and answer with a partner.

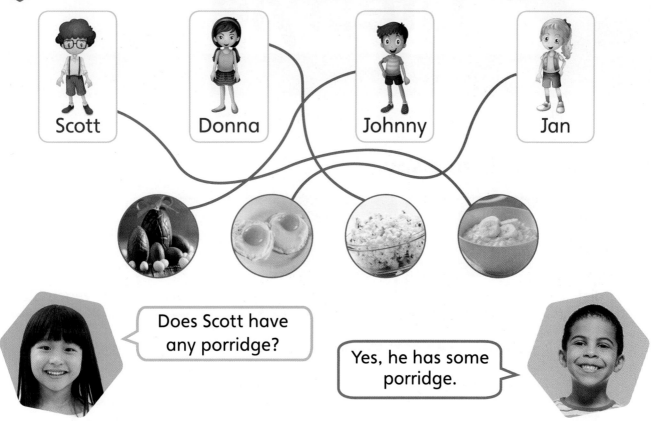

Scott   Donna   Johnny   Jan

Does Scott have any porridge?

Yes, he has some porridge.

9 **Read and match. Then listen and check.**

a Let's make a pizza for dinner.

Great! I can make the tomato sauce.

b Yes, there are. There are six tomatoes in the fridge.

I like it too! And we've got some ice cream for dessert!

c Okay, good idea. Do we have any mushrooms?

That sounds good. Are there any tomatoes?

d Cheese and tomato pizza is my favorite!

No, we don't. But we have some cheese.

 THINK BIG

Imagine you're making lunch for a friend. What do you need? Make a shopping list.

8 A Better Lifestyle

1 Listen, look, and say.

 1 diet

 2 exercise

 3 rooftop garden

 4 plants

 5 vegetables

 6 exhaust fumes

 7 fresh air

 8 race

 9 bunk beds

2 Read and complete.

> fresh   vegetables   race   fumes   diet   exercise

a Do some _____ for 30 minutes a day.

b Try growing _____ and other plants.

c Try to follow a healthy _____.

d Go out and get lots of _____ air every day.

e Wear a mask when you go cycling, so you don't breathe in exhaust _____.

f Run fast so you can win the _____!

3 🎧 **Listen, look, and say.**

| ready-made | fit | healthy | unhealthy |

4 **What can you do to stay healthy? Draw. Then ask and answer with a partner.**

water

exercise

diet

vegetables

sport

fresh air

5 **Watch. What do you hear or see? Number the pictures, 1 to 6.**

6 **Watch again. Then read and complete.**

bunk beds　　garden　　offices　　oxygen　　race

a People in _____ spend a long time sitting down.

b In an office in Japan, you can sleep on _____.

c A rooftop _____ can be relaxing.

d Gardens put _____ into the air.

e The _____ in Moscow is up 195 steps!

7 **Read and circle. Then listen and check.**

People in **gardens / offices** spend a long time sitting down, their eyes glued to a **TV / computer** screen. Many people have no choice but to have a quick, usually ready-made **breakfast / lunch** at their desk. That's not the best way of eating **healthy / unhealthy** food. Others have to work late **in the morning / at night**.

8 **Follow the paths. Ask and answer with a partner.**

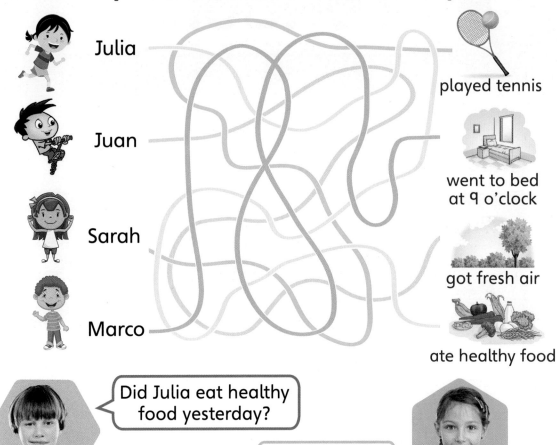

Julia

Juan

Sarah

Marco

played tennis

went to bed at 9 o'clock

got fresh air

ate healthy food

Did Julia eat healthy food yesterday?

Yes, she did.

9 **Read and match.**

a Did Mom and Dad get enough exercise?

b Did she get enough fresh air?

c Did they get enough healthy food yesterday?

d Did he get enough rest yesterday?

No, they didn't.

No, he didn't. He's tired.

Yes, they did. They ran a race!

Yes, she did.

THINK BIG Do your classmates get enough fresh air and exercise? Make a chart.

A Day in London

I will learn about going on school trips.

 1 Listen, number, and say.

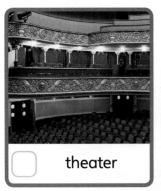
◯ theater

◯ church

◯ gallery

◯ museum

◯ park

◯ cathedral

◯ exhibition

2 Read and complete.

park	museum	gallery	cathedral	theater

a The main church in a city. _____

b Green land where you can play or exercise. _____

c A place where interesting objects are shown. _____

d A room where people look at art. _____

e A place where plays or concerts are performed. _____

🎧 33 3 Look, read, and match. Then listen and check.

 a

 b

 c

(steps)　(slide)　(staircase)

4 What place would you like to visit? What interesting things can you see there? Draw. Then ask answer with a partner.

5 ►vq **Watch. Check (✓) what you hear or see.**

☐ galleries   ☐ steps   ☐ the Queen

☐ cathedral   ☐ staircases   ☐ Buckingham Palace

☐ parks   ☐ theatre   ☐ slides

☐ museums

6 ►vq **Watch again. Answer the questions.**

a How long did it take to complete the Royal Academy staircase?

_____

b What is hidden in the walls of Saint Paul's Cathedral?

_____

c Does the canopy stair help people climb trees?

_____

d How many slides are there at the Science Museum?

_____

7 🎧 34 **Read and complete. Then listen and check.**

museums	field	summer	staircase	hours

Today, we are going on a _____ trip to
London. We will visit galleries, churches, parks, and
_____. In each one, we're going to take a look
at their steps and staircases. We find a psychedelic
_____ at the Royal Academy. It took 500
_____ and lots of sticky tape to complete. It
leads up to a very colorful _____ exhibition.

8 **Follow the lines. Ask and answer with a partner.**

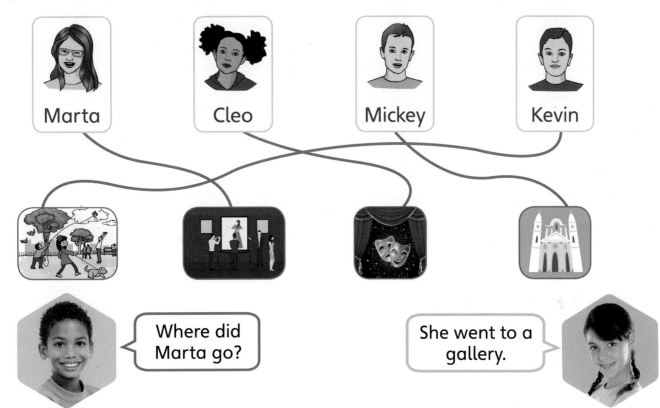

Marta | Cleo | Mickey | Kevin

Where did Marta go?

She went to a gallery.

9 **Write the words in order and match. Then listen and check.**

a did - Bob - go - Where - Sally - and?

Where did Sally and Bob go?

Yes, he did. He said it was interesting.

b see - did - What - they?

_____

They went to a gallery.

c it - Bob - Did - like?

_____

No, she didn't. She said it was boring.

d Sally - like - too - Did - it?

_____

They saw a photo exhibition.

THINK BIG

Where did your classmates go on vacation last year? Make a chart.

Word List

❶ Staying Clean

brush your teeth
don't pass on germs
have a bath
keep clean
sneeze into your hands
take a shower
wash your hands
bacteria
dirt
hot spring
insect
minerals

❷ Trains

elevated train
monorail
passenger
railway
station
ticket
ticket inspector
underground train
model train
the Tube
tourists

❸ Working Together

communicate with
develop a bond with
feed
jump out of
trust
work with
farmer
horse whisperer
mahout

❹ Hidden Animals

chameleon
cuttlefish
frogfish
goat
gorilla
octopus
shrimp
snow leopard
paw prints
pebble
seaweed
shells

❺ Extreme Weather

freezing
icy
rainy
snowy
stormy
sunny
warm
windy
deep
extreme

❻ The Senses

hear
radar
see
smell
sonar
taste
touch
bat
bottlenose dolphin
hammerhead shark
stingray

❼ What's Cooking?

bake
cook
crack
eat
fry
make
fried egg
popcorn
porridge

❽ A Better Lifestyle

bunk beds
diet
exercise
exhaust fumes
fresh air
plants
race
rooftop garden
vegetables
fit
healthy
ready-made
unhealthy

❾ A Day in London

cathedral
church
exhibition
gallery
museum
park
theater
slide
staircase
steps